30 Days to Debt Confidence

Rewriting Your Debt Story with Clarity, Control, and Courage

by

Tamra S. Connor, Ph.D.

Notes

For permissions, inquiries, or educator resources, visit:
https://www.tamraconnor.com

First Edition

ISBN: 979-8-950867-02-6

Cover + Interior Design: TnT WayPoints Creative

Published by TnT Waypoints Publishing, USA

This book is for educational and motivational purposes. The stories, examples, and scenarios reflect common financial experiences, but every reader's situation is unique. The author and publisher make no guarantees and assume no liability for decisions made based on this material.

TnT Waypoints, LLC is committed to empowering individuals and educators with practical, accessible tools that build lifelong financial strength, one intentional step at a time.

Printed in the United States of America

Notes

Introduction

Debt has a way of affecting far more than our finances. It can influence our decisions, limit our opportunities, disrupt our peace of mind, and create uncertainty about the future. Whether it comes from student loans, credit cards, medical bills, personal loans, or years of financial setbacks, debt often carries an emotional weight that feels just as heavy as the numbers on a statement.

If you are holding this book, chances are you are ready for something different. Not another complicated financial system; not another lecture about what you should have done years ago; and not another promise of overnight wealth. What you need is confidence.

30 Days to Debt Confidence was written to help you develop a healthier, stronger, and more intentional relationship with debt and money. Confidence does not come from having a perfect financial situation. It comes from understanding where you are, knowing what steps to take next, and believing that consistent action can create meaningful change.

As part of the **TnT WayPoints Series**, this book is built on a simple but powerful principle: lasting transformation occurs one waypoint at a time. Every meaningful journey has markers that help travelers understand where they are, measure their progress, and keep moving forward. Financial freedom is no different.

Over the next 30 days, you will encounter practical lessons, reflective exercises, and actionable strategies designed to help you:

- Understand your current debt situation without fear or shame.
- Develop a clear picture of your financial reality.
- Create manageable plans for reducing debt.

- Build habits that support long-term financial health.
- Strengthen your mindset around money and personal responsibility.
- Replace anxiety with clarity and uncertainty with purpose.

This is not a book about perfection. It is a book about progress.

Some days will challenge you to confront financial decisions you have avoided. Other days will encourage you as you recognize strengths you may have overlooked. Each step is designed to build momentum because confidence grows through action, and action becomes sustainable when broken into manageable pieces.

The **TnT Waypoints Series** is founded on the belief that meaningful change happens when knowledge meets intentional practice. Reading alone will not change your financial future. Applying what you learn will. That is why this book invites you to engage actively with each day's waypoint, take an honest inventory of your circumstances, and commit to the small but significant decisions that build financial resilience.

No matter where you begin, remember this: debt does not define your worth. Your financial challenges are part of your story, but they are not the end of it. With patience, discipline, and a willingness to take one step at a time, you can move from confusion to clarity, from stress to confidence, and from feeling trapped by debt to taking control of your financial future.

Welcome to your journey.

Welcome to **30 Days to Debt Confidence.** Your next waypoint begins today!

How to Use This Book

Each day includes:

- A simple challenge
- A short lesson to help you understand the "why."
- Reflection prompts deepening your awareness
- An original inspirational quote to anchor the day

You can complete one challenge per day or stretch them out. What matters is consistency. This is your guide, your journal, your accountability partner, and your reset, all in one.

Let's begin!

Facing Debt with Clarity

Turn on the lights. See the truth. Face the Numbers.

Before debt can be reduced or eliminated, it must be faced honestly. That sounds simple, but for many people, this is the hardest part. Debt hides in the corners of our lives, in the unopened statements, avoided balances, and assumptions that keep us guessing. Sometimes guilt gets in the way. Sometimes overwhelm does. And sometimes we simply don't know where to begin.

Clarity changes everything. When you turn on a light in a dark room, the obstacles that once felt intimidating become visible and manageable. Debt works the same way. Clarity replaces assumptions with facts, anxiety with understanding, and fear with a plan. It gives you an accurate picture of your financial reality, not to judge yourself, but to move forward with confidence.

This section builds that foundation. You'll examine your current financial situation, identify the debts you owe, and explore the habits and beliefs shaping your decisions. Most importantly, you'll learn to view your circumstances with objectivity instead of emotion.

Awareness is not failure. It's freedom. Every successful debt journey begins with someone willing to stop avoiding the numbers and start engaging with them. You don't need all the answers or a perfect past, only the courage to look honestly at where you are.

The goal of this section isn't discouragement. It's confidence. Once you clearly see where you stand, you can begin charting a path toward where you want to go.

This is your first waypoint. Take a breath. Open the books. Gather the facts. Let's face debt with clarity.

Let's face debt with clarity.

DAY 1

Define What Debt Confidence Means to You

When you first think about your debt, you may feel overwhelmed or even lost. You may not know what confidence looks like either. Once you can define it, you have something to work toward.

As you sit down to think about your debt, you expect to feel motivated. Instead, you feel uncertain. You want things to be different, but you struggle to describe what "better" actually looks like.

Maybe you imagine the day every balance is paid off. Maybe you picture opening your banking app without anxiety. Perhaps debt confidence means having a plan, staying on budget, or knowing your financial future is no longer controlled by past decisions.

You may realize your biggest challenge isn't the debt itself but the lack of a clear destination. It's hard to make progress when you don't know where you're trying to go.

Debt confidence looks different for everyone. For one person, it's freedom from credit cards. For another, it's sleeping peacefully knowing bills are under control. For someone else, it's making financial decisions without fear, shame, or confusion.

Today isn't about solving your debt. It's about defining the future you want. When you can picture what debt confidence means to you, every decision gains purpose and direction.

Confidence doesn't appear when your debt hits zero. It's built along the way, starting the moment you decide what you're working toward.

"Confidence begins with clarity."

Why This Matters

Many people focus so much on eliminating debt that they never define the life they hope to create after it is gone. As a result, their financial journey feels like an endless sacrifice rather than meaningful progress.

Your personal definition of debt confidence becomes a guiding waypoint. It helps you stay motivated during challenging moments and reminds you why your efforts matter. The clearer your vision, the easier it becomes to recognize progress and celebrate small victories along the way.

You cannot build confidence without first deciding what confidence means to you.

The Challenge

Write your personal definition of debt confidence. Complete the following statement: Debt confidence means ____. Then expand your answer by writing two or three sentences describing how your life would look and feel if you achieved that definition.

Reflection

What would feeling confident about your debt look like? What habits do you think a confident person would practice consistently?

Your WayPoint Takeaway

Debt confidence is not someone else's goal. It is your goal, defined by your values, priorities, and vision for the future. Today's task creates the destination for the journey ahead.

Before you can start the path, you must first decide where you want to go. Today, you began your journey towards debt confidence.

DAY 2

Identify Your Emotional Debt Story

You probably are not afraid of the numbers, but you may be afraid of what you believe the numbers say about you.

You sit down with a pen and paper, ready to tell the truth about your relationship with debt. You may want to focus on balances and interest rates, but today is about the story behind them.

Think about your earliest memories of money and what you learned growing up. Was it a source of security or stress? Was it openly discussed or avoided? These early messages often shape how you handle debt today. Maybe you learned that debt was normal, that success required owning more, or that asking for help meant failure.

Write down the moments that influenced your debt journey. You might remember your first credit card, an emergency that required borrowing, student loans taken with hope, or spending during stressful seasons. Patterns will appear. Some debt came from necessity, some from optimism, some from fear or expectations.

Then consider the story you have been telling yourself about your debt. Thoughts like never getting ahead or being bad with money can feel true, but they are beliefs, not facts. The fact is that you have debt. The story is what you decided that debt means about you.

Debt may be part of your history, but it does not define your identity.

Take a breath and write a new ending. You are learning to eliminate debt. You are building stronger habits. Every payment moves you closer to freedom.

"Your debt is a situation, not a judgment."

Why This Matters

Before you can create a plan to eliminate debt, you need to understand the beliefs, experiences, and habits that helped create it. Many people focus only on the numbers, but debt is often driven by a deeper story about money, success, security, self-worth, or scarcity.

If you don't identify the story behind your debt, you may continue repeating the same financial patterns even after paying off balances. Lasting financial change happens when you understand not only **what** decisions you've made, but also **why** you've made them.

Emotions shape your decision more than numbers do. Today, you begin to understand the emotions behind your money decisions.

The Challenge

Write down the emotions you associate with your debt. Before beginning today's reflection, respond to these prompts:

My debt story began when

____

____

____

____

The beliefs I have carried about debt are

The financial habits that contributed to my debt are

The story I want to tell going forward is

Reflection

What is the most important insight you gained about your debt story, and how can that insight help you make different financial choices in the future?

Your WayPoint Takeaway

Your debt story is not your identity. The financial decisions, circumstances, and experiences that led to your debt are part of your story, but they do not define who you are. By identifying the beliefs and patterns behind your debt, you gain the awareness needed to create lasting change. When you understand the story driving your financial choices, you can begin replacing limiting beliefs with empowering ones and take intentional steps toward financial freedom.

Awareness creates choice, and choice creates change. Your debt may be part of your past, but it does not have to determine your future.

DAY 3

Face the Numbers

Your income is the foundation of your financial life. Before you build anything, you need to know exactly what you're working with.

You open your laptop and hesitate. For months, you have avoided looking at your debt, convincing yourself that not seeing it made it easier to manage. Yet the uncertainty follows you whenever you check your bank account or think about your future. Today is different.

You take a breath and begin gathering information. One by one, you open balances, loan statements, and credit card accounts. It feels uncomfortable at first, but as the numbers appear, something shifts. The more you learn, the less powerless you feel.

Write down each debt with its balance, interest rate, and minimum payment. Slowly, the picture becomes clearer. Some balances are higher than you expected, others lower, and a few were causing far more stress simply because you never looked closely.

You start to see that the truth is less frightening than the stories you created. Your relationship with your debt begins to change. The numbers are not perfect, but they are no longer a mystery.

For the first time, you can see your full financial landscape. You know where you stand, and because you know where you stand, you can choose where you are going.

Today, you replace avoidance with awareness. Today, fear gives way to clarity. And clarity creates direction.

"You cannot change what you refuse to see."

Why This Matters

Many people think debt is the problem, but the real obstacle is often avoidance. When you do not know how much you owe, your mind fills the gaps with fear and worst-case scenarios. The unknown becomes heavier than reality.

Facing your debt may feel uncomfortable, but clarity is powerful. Once you know the numbers, you stop guessing and start planning. You move from feeling overwhelmed to feeling informed. Instead of carrying vague stress, you gain a clear picture of what you are working with and where you want to go.

This exercise is not about judgment. It is simply gathering facts like balances, interest rates, and minimum payments. The clearer your financial picture becomes, the more confidently you can take your next step.

Clarity turns fear into direction.

The Challenge

List every debt: balance, interest rate, and minimum payment.

Description of the Debt	Balance	Interest Rate	Minimum Payment

Reflection

What surprised you most about seeing all your debts listed in one place, and how did it change the way you feel about your financial situation?

____

____

____

____

____

____

____

____

Your WayPoint Takeaway

Avoiding your debt may feel safer for a moment, but uncertainty often creates more stress than the numbers themselves. Facing the numbers replaces fear with facts and overwhelm with understanding.

Listing every balance, interest rate, and minimum payment gives you a clear starting point. You cannot build a plan around what you have not measured.

Debt grows in the dark but loses power in the light. Every financial success story begins with honesty. By facing the numbers today, you have taken an important step from avoidance to action and from uncertainty to confidence.

DAY 4

Identify Your Debt Types

Review your list from yesterday. Not all your debts are the same. Some debt is strategic, some accidental, and some simply outdated.

At first glance, your list feels like one giant mountain to climb. Every balance seems to blend, creating a sense of overwhelming anxiety.

But today, you are going to take a closer look.

Review each debt one by one. As you do, you realize that each has a different story. One debt helped pay for a future career opportunity, while another allowed you to purchase reliable transportation. Some debts were unexpected, such as those from the accident that led to medical expenses. Other debts may have accumulated from everyday spending, emergencies, or financial decisions made during difficult seasons of your life.

As you review your debts, you begin to see them differently. The credit card debt, carrying a high interest rate, may require immediate attention. The student loan debt may have a longer repayment timeline. The medical debt may reflect a situation you never anticipated.

Each debt has its own story, cost, and level of urgency. By labeling your debts, you aren't making excuses for them. Instead, you are creating understanding. The more clearly you understand what you owe, the more effectively you can decide what to do next.

And with every category you create,
your path forward becomes a little clearer.

"Not all debt carries the same weight."

Why This Matters

People often see debt as one big problem, but each type of debt is different. A student loan, credit card balance, medical bill, and auto loan all come with their own interest rates, terms, risks, and long-term effects.

Understanding what kinds of debt you have helps you make smarter repayment choices. Some debts require attention due to high interest rates, while others offer more flexible terms or long-term benefits. Categorizing your debt gives you a clearer view of your financial situation and helps you create a strategy that fits your goals.

Instead of seeing one overwhelming burden, you begin to see individual obligations, each with its own path forward.

The Challenge

Select an appropriate category for each, such as credit card/high-interest, student loans, auto loans, medical loans, personal loans, mortgage loans, family/friend loans, etc.

With every category you create, your path forward becomes a little clearer.

Description of the Debt	Balance	Interest Rate	Minimum Payment	Type of Debt

Reflection

Looking at your debt categories, which type of debt feels most urgent to address, and why does it stand out to you?

Your WayPoint Takeaway

Not all debt affects your financial life the same way. When you identify and categorize each debt, you can see which ones need attention now and which can be managed over time. Viewing all debt as a single heavy burden can make it feel like you're stuck, but separating it into clear groups reveals priorities and strategies. What once felt like a single mountain becomes a series of manageable steps.

Every debt has a story, a purpose, and a path to repayment. The clearer you understand each one, the more effectively you can create a plan to eliminate it. Awareness brings clarity and helps you focus your energy where it matters most.

DAY 5

Calculate Your
Total Monthly Debt Payments

You know what debts you owe. You know the types of debt you carry. Now it's time to understand how those debts affect your monthly cash flow.

You glance at your list of debts and feel a familiar heaviness. A credit card payment is coming, the student loan drafts each month, the car payment appears as usual, and maybe medical or personal loans sit in the mix. Each one seems manageable on its own, but today you are looking at the full picture.

For years, it may have felt like debt was consuming your income, yet you never added up how much you pay each month. When you finally total everything, you may feel surprise followed by clarity. The number might be significant, but it is no longer unknown.

For the first time, you can see exactly how much of your income goes toward debt. You understand why certain goals feel out of reach and where your money is going. You also see that eliminating every debt puts money back in your pocket.

As you add the amounts, you may feel discouraged, relieved, or motivated. Whatever you feel, stay present with the number. It is not a judgment. It is information. It reflects your current reality, not your future.

This total marks the beginning of your strategy. Every debt you pay off reduces the burden. Every extra payment moves you closer to freedom. Every decision now rests on a clear understanding of your finances. Today, you stop guessing and gain clarity. Clarity gives you the power to create a plan.

"Numbers bring truth. Truth brings control."

Why This Matters

You know what debts you owe. You know the types of debt you carry. Now it's time to understand how those debts affect your monthly cash flow.

Many people focus on total balances and overlook the amount of money leaving their accounts each month to maintain those debts. Yet your monthly debt payments directly affect your ability to save, invest, build an emergency fund, and pursue your financial goals.

When you calculate your total monthly debt payments, you gain a clearer picture of where your money is going. This number becomes the foundation for your debt repayment strategy and helps you identify opportunities to free up cash and accelerate your progress.

Knowledge creates confidence. When you know the number, you can begin making informed decisions instead of relying on assumptions.

The Challenge

Calculate your total monthly debt payments by adding together the minimum payment for each debt you owe.

My Total Monthly Debt Payments: $____________________

This number is the foundation of your plan.

Reflection

How does seeing your total monthly debt payments in one place make you feel, and what does this number reveal about your current financial priorities?

Your WayPoint Takeaway

Calculating your total monthly debt payments reveals more than a number. It shows how much of your income is tied to past obligations and how much freedom you can gain as those debts are paid off. Many people feel overwhelmed because they never see the full monthly impact. By adding up your required payments, you turn uncertainty into understanding. You now know exactly what debt costs you each month, and that knowledge becomes a tool for change.

What gets measured gets managed. Your total monthly debt payment is the starting point for your financial freedom plan. Today you gained clarity. Soon you will use that clarity to make intentional choices that move you toward your goals.

DAY 6
Identify Your Debt Triggers

You look back at your debt list and wonder how some of the balances became so large.

Debt builds one decision at a time. Purchases may seem random, but once you look closely, patterns begin to appear. Stress, exhaustion, convenience, or the desire for relief often influence moments when credit feels easier than finding another solution.

Start paying attention to what usually happens before you use credit. Stress, boredom, celebration, pressure, or the desire for a reward can all be triggers. Sometimes the trigger is convenience or lack of time. Sometimes, unexpected expenses catch you off guard because a financial cushion is not yet in place. Certain stores, websites, or social media ads can also make spending feel almost automatic.

This exercise is not about blame. It is about understanding your habits. Each trigger you identify gives you a chance to choose a different response, whether managing emotions, building a small buffer, or finding alternatives to impulse spending.

The goal is awareness. Debt is shaped by patterns, and once you recognize a pattern, you gain the power to change it.

"Debt has triggers.
Confidence comes from knowing them."

Why This Matters

Debt rarely happens by accident. While unexpected emergencies can create financial challenges, many spending decisions are influenced by habits, emotions, situations, and routines that repeat over time.

Understanding your debt triggers helps you move beyond focusing solely on the money and begin examining the behaviors behind it. When you identify the circumstances that lead you to rely on credit, you gain the ability to make different choices before debt accumulates.

Awareness creates a pause between the trigger and the action. In that pause, you can choose a response that supports your financial goals rather than working against them.

The Challenge

Identify the situations, emotions, or circumstances that most often lead you to use credit. Consider things like:

- Stress or anxiety
- Unexpected expenses
- Time pressures or convenience
- Social events or peer pressure
- Celebrations or rewards
- Boredom
- Emotional Spending
- Lack of planning or budgeting
- Habits
- Other personal triggers

Reflection

What are your top three debt triggers? Which one feels most familiar to you? What is one action you could take to interrupt that pattern the next time it appears?

Your WayPoint Takeaway

Debt behaviors often begin long before a credit card is used. They grow from emotions, habits, and situations that influence your choices. By identifying your triggers, you have taken an important step toward understanding why you spend.

Awareness gives you the chance to respond differently. When you recognize the moments that tempt you to rely on credit, you can prepare healthier habits and make choices that support your long-term goals.

You cannot always prevent a trigger, but you can choose your response. The more aware you are of your patterns, the more control you gain. Every trigger you identify is an opportunity to break a cycle, strengthen a habit, and move closer to financial freedom.

DAY 7

Celebrate Your Progress

One week ago, you began this journey. Today, you celebrate that beginning.

You may have started with uncertainty. Maybe you felt overwhelmed by your debt, anxious about your finances, or unsure whether change was even possible. The road ahead might have felt long, and the numbers may have seemed intimidating. **But look at what you've accomplished.**

You took an honest look at your debt story. You faced numbers you may have been avoiding. You organized your debts and began to understand them. You calculated what debt is costing you each month. You identified the patterns and triggers that influence your financial decisions. Most importantly, you showed up. Day after day. Even when the exercises felt uncomfortable. Even when the answers weren't easy. Even when you would have rather looked away.

You chose awareness over avoidance, and that deserves recognition.

Everything changes when you stop measuring success only by how much debt remains and start recognizing the actions you consistently take. The more you celebrate progress, the more motivated you will be to continue.

Financial freedom is built one decision, one habit, and one day at a time. This week was not about perfection. It was about progress.

And you've already begun creating a different financial future.

"Progress deserves to be celebrated, not postponed."

Why This Matters

Many people focus so much on how far they still have to go that they overlook how much progress they have already made. Financial growth is not only about paying off balances. It is also about awareness, new habits, and the courage to face your situation.

This week, you did meaningful work. You examined your debt story, faced the numbers, organized your debts, calculated your obligations, and identified the triggers that shape your decisions. These steps are the foundation for lasting change.

Celebrating your progress builds momentum. When you acknowledge your wins, you remind yourself that growth is happening even before the balances begin to shrink.

The Challenge

Celebrate completing the first week. Identify three things you have learned about our finances this week. What are three accomplishments you are proud of from this week? And, what is one positive financial habit you want to continue building?

Reflection

Looking back on your first week, what accomplishment are you most proud of, and how has your perspective of your financial journey changed since Day 1?

Your WayPoint Takeaway

You don't have to wait until you are debt-free to recognize your growth. Every honest conversation, every number you face, every habit you examine, and every step you take toward financial awareness is a victory.

Remember: Financial freedom is not built in a single moment. It's built through consistent actions over time. This week, you proved to yourself that you are willing to face your finances with honesty and courage. That's something worth celebrating, and it's a strong foundation for everything that comes next.

From Clarity to Control

This week, you chose awareness over avoidance. You took an honest look at your debt, uncovered the emotions and beliefs behind it, and gained a clear picture of where you stand. You were never expected to solve every financial challenge in seven days. Your goal was clarity, and you achieved it. Next week, you will begin turning that clarity into confidence and action.

You cannot build a financial plan on uncertainty. Before you set priorities or accelerate progress, you need to know what you are working with. This week gave you that foundation. You now understand your debt story, your numbers, your obligations, and the patterns that influence your decisions. These insights matter because they support every step that comes next.

As you move into **Section 2: Building Control and Structure**, your focus shifts from awareness to action. Instead of looking backward at how debt formed, you will look forward at how to eliminate it. You will learn to organize your finances, create supportive systems, and build a clear roadmap for paying down debt with purpose.

Control does not come from perfect finances. It comes from having a plan. And structure creates freedom.

You spent the last seven days building awareness. Now you will build the habits, systems, and confidence that turn awareness into lasting progress.

Take a moment to celebrate how far you have come. Then get ready for what is next.

DAY 8

Choose Your Debt Strategy

Choosing your debt payoff strategy is the moment you stop reacting to your debt and start directing it.

Until now, your payments may have felt scattered. You paid a little on one card, put a bill on another, and focused only on what was due next. A strategy changes that. It gives your effort direction and turns randomness into momentum.

Snowball and **Avalanche** are the two proven approaches. Both work. What matters is choosing the one that fits your personality and motivation style.

Snowball focuses on the smallest debt first. It is fast, visible, and builds confidence. Each cleared balance creates a win, which helps you stay motivated.

Avalanche targets the highest interest rate first. It is efficient and saves the most money over time. If you value logic and long-term payoff, it keeps you focused.

Neither method is better. The best strategy is the one you will follow. Debt freedom comes from consistency. Choosing your method means choosing the path that aligns with your strengths and habits.

"The best strategy is the one you can sustain."

Why This Matters

Strategy gives you direction because it turns intention into a path you can follow. Without a strategy, your effort scatters, and you pay whatever bill feels urgent, react to whatever balance screams the loudest, and hope progress shows up. A strategy changes that. It gives your decisions a purpose, your payments a sequence, and your momentum a shape. When you choose a debt strategy, you're not just deciding *how* to pay off debt; you're deciding *where you're going* and *how you'll get there*. It's the difference between wandering and moving with intention.

The Challenge

Choose the strategy that will work best for you.

Reflection

Why did you choose this strategy? Why do you think it is the one that you will stick with?

Your WayPoint Takeaway

A strategy is your turning point. It is the moment you stop drifting and start directing your debt payoff with intention. Once you choose your path, every payment becomes purposeful, every step builds momentum, and the way forward becomes clear.

DAY 9

Create a Debt Priority List

Today, clarity meets action. You will create your own roadmap to pay off your debts.

Up until now, your debts may have lived in the background, scattered across statements, apps, emails, and mental notes you try not to think about. Putting them into one organized list changes that. It brings your debt into a structure you control.

Creating a priority list is more than writing down balances. It is arranging your financial reality in a way that makes sense to you. You decide what matters most, what needs attention first, and what can wait. This list becomes the backbone of your strategy and the map that shows where you stand and where you are heading.

As you rank your debts, patterns appear. You see which balances drain money through high interest, which ones are small enough to clear quickly, and which obligations carry emotional weight. Your list captures all of it. It is honest, personal, and powerful.

Once everything is laid out, the path forward becomes clearer. You know what to tackle, what to monitor, and what to celebrate. A priority list does not erase your debt, but it removes confusion, and clarity builds confidence.

This is the moment your debt stops being a pile of numbers and becomes a plan. Your priority list is your roadmap, and every step from here moves you closer to freedom.

"Order creates calm."

Why This Matters

Prioritization reduces the overwhelming feeling of being in debt. Your priority list matters because it replaces uncertainty with clarity. When all your debts are laid out in one place, they can be organized, ranked, and visible. You finally see the full picture instead of guessing your way through it. Clarity reduces stress, sharpens your strategy, and helps you make decisions with confidence instead of hesitation. A priority list turns scattered obligations into a structured plan, giving you control over what happens next.

You can't control what you don't acknowledge.

The Challenge

Using the table created last week, rank your debts based on your chosen strategy.

Rank	Description of the Debt	Balance	Interest Rate	Minimum Payment	Type of Debt

Reflection

Which debt feels most motivating to tackle? Where does it rank on your priority list?

Your WayPoint Takeaway

A debt priority list gives you control by turning scattered obligations into a clear, organized plan. When you know exactly what comes first, what comes next, and why each step matters, you move with confidence rather than confusion, and that clarity becomes the fuel for real progress.

DAY 10

Review Your Credit Report

You don't need to make huge extra payments, just consistent ones.

A minimum-plus plan is where your debt payoff stops being accidental and becomes intentional. Every debt has a minimum payment, but minimums only keep you afloat; they don't move you forward. A minimum-plus plan gives you a simple, realistic structure you can stick to.

You start by choosing a monthly amount you can truly commit to that fits your real life. That's your baseline. Then you add a small, steady "plus" that builds momentum. That extra $10, $25, or $50 is what turns slow progress into real progress.

The strength of this plan is consistency. You're not waiting for a bonus or a lucky break; you're building progress into your routine. You prove you can move forward even when life is busy or money feels tight. That small "plus" becomes your commitment to the future you — the one who deserves less stress and more freedom.

This plan isn't flashy, but it works. Every month, you do more than the minimum, pushing your debt in the right direction and building a habit that compounds over time. Progress doesn't require perfection; it requires intention.

A minimum-plus plan is simple, sustainable, and powerful. It's the moment you stop hoping your debt will shrink and start making it happen.

"Small extra payments create big long-term impact."

Why This Matters

A minimum-plus plan matters because consistency is what builds momentum. When you commit to a set amount every month and then add a little extra, you create a steady push that keeps your debt moving in the right direction. That small "plus" may not feel dramatic in the moment, but over time it compounds and shrinks balances faster, strengthening your habits, and proving that progress doesn't come from big leaps, but from repeated, intentional steps. This is how you turn effort into acceleration.

It is your chance to take the necessary steps to rewrite your future.

The Challenge

Commit to paying that little extra to the highest-ranked debt on your list. Why is this important to you?

Reflection

What monthly amount feels sustainable enough to stick with and strong enough to make progress?

Your Waypoint Takeaway

A minimum-plus plan turns consistency into momentum. By committing to a steady monthly amount and adding a small, intentional "plus," you create a pattern of progress that builds month after month. It's a simple structure that keeps you moving forward, proving that disciplined steps, even small ones, lead to meaningful change.

DAY 11

Identify Your Debt Barriers

Debt isn't a math problem; it is a behavior problem, a mindset problem, a life-circumstance problem.

Before you can move forward with your debt plan, you need to understand what has been holding you back. Barriers shape your choices long before you notice them, and identifying them is how you regain control.

Debt barriers come in many forms. Some are practical, like irregular income, high living costs, medical bills, or emergencies that drain savings. Others are emotional, such as fear of facing the numbers, shame about past decisions, or the belief that you will never get ahead.

Naming your barriers removes their power. You stop seeing them as personal failures and start seeing them as obstacles you can navigate. This step is not about judgment. It is about clarity. You acknowledge the forces that shaped your financial path so you can redirect it.

As you explore your barriers, patterns appear. You notice where stress triggers spending. You see which expenses derail progress. You recognize the stories that kept you stuck, and once you see them, you can challenge them.

Identifying your debt barriers is an act of honesty and courage. It is the moment you stop fighting blind. You are not just preparing to pay off debt. You are preparing to remove the roadblocks that kept you from financial freedom. This awareness sharpens your strategy, strengthens your discipline, and reminds you that every barrier can be overcome once it is brought into the light.

"Barriers aren't failures. They are information."

Why This Matters

You cannot fix what you cannot see. Identifying debt barriers gives you clarity about the forces that shape your financial decisions and limit your options. Without naming them, any debt plan relies on guesswork, keeping people stuck.

Debt pressure reduces flexibility because interest costs shrink your income and limit saving and long-term goals.

Barriers explain why debt feels overwhelming. The problem is not only the balances. It is the drag that debt creates across your entire financial system.

Unidentified barriers lead to distress, including missed payments, reliance on credit for daily expenses, lower credit scores, and reduced financial stability.

Most people face at least one major obstacle, often high expenses, high debt, or low income.

The Challenge

List the obstacles that make paying debt difficult.

____

____

____

____

____

____

Reflection

Which barriers feel easiest to solve? Hardest?

Your Waypoint Takeaway

Identifying your debt barriers is the moment you stop fighting in the dark. When you name what's been blocking your progress, including the habits, the pressures, the emotions, and the circumstances, you turn confusion into clarity. Barriers lose their power once they're visible, and clarity becomes the compass that guides every decision you make from here.

DAY 12
Build a Debt Buffer

A debt buffer is your breathing room. It's the small cushion that keeps life from knocking your debt plan off track every time something unexpected happens.

Without a buffer, even small surprises like a co-pay or car repair can push you back into using credit, and once you return to that cycle, it becomes harder to escape.

A debt buffer is not a full emergency fund. It provides enough space for your payoff plan to survive real life. You choose a realistic monthly amount to set aside, then add a small extra amount. Even five or ten dollars turns a simple habit into protection.

As your buffer grows, you stop panicking at unexpected expenses and stop relying on credit for every problem. You make decisions based on stability rather than stress, which keeps your debt plan moving even when life is unpredictable.

A buffer is more than money. It is confidence and control. It prepares you for bumps in the road and shifts your mindset from hoping things go smoothly to planning for challenges.

This buffer becomes your safety net and momentum protector. Every dollar strengthens your foundation, every month reinforces discipline, and every wise use keeps your payoff journey moving forward.

"A buffer protects your progress."

Why This Matters

A debt buffer matters because it protects your progress. Without a cushion, every unexpected expense becomes a setback that pushes you back toward credit, interest, and stress. Even a small buffer gives you stability, reduces financial pressure, and keeps your debt-reduction plan moving forward. It's not about building a big fund. It's about creating enough breathing room so life can happen without undoing your hard work.

The Challenge

Choose the exact amount you will set aside for your debt buffer, then automate it! Make it a non-negotiable part of your monthly cash flow.

Write down the amount you will set aside for your debt buffer, and how you plan to automate it.

Reflection

How does having a buffer change your confidence? How could having a buffer help reduce your financial stress and increase the confidence you are building?

Your Waypoint Takeaway

A debt buffer is your momentum protector. It keeps life's surprises from undoing your progress and gives you the breathing room to stay consistent even when things get messy. This small cushion becomes the difference between relying on credit and relying on yourself.

DAY 13

Review Your Interest Rates

Interest rates are the quiet force shaping your debt story.

Interest rates determine how fast your balances grow, how much of each payment reduces your principal, and how long it takes to become debt-free. If you do not know your rates, you are navigating blind and working hard without working smart.

Reviewing your rates gives you visibility. It shows which debts cost the most and which quietly drain your future. Some rates are manageable; others are harmful. Some balances barely move even with regular payments, while others respond quickly once you focus on them. Clear numbers allow you to prioritize with intention instead of guesswork.

This step is a strategy, not a judgment. You gather information to see where your money has the greatest impact, which debts need to be addressed urgently, and which can wait. You learn the true cost of carrying debt, including interest that compounds month after month.

As you review your rates, patterns appear. You see which debts grow in the background, where minimum payments barely help, and which accounts hold you back. With that clarity, you can build a payoff plan that accelerates progress.

Reviewing your interest rates is a moment of clarity. It sharpens your strategy, increases efficiency, and aligns your plan with your goals. You are not just paying off debt. You are learning how to outsmart it.

"Interest is the silent cost of debt."

Why This Matters

Interest determines the true cost of your debt. When you know your rates, you can prioritize the balances that drain your money the fastest, reduce long-term costs, and shorten your payoff timeline. Without this clarity, you risk putting effort into the wrong places and losing momentum. Reviewing your interest rates ensures every dollar you pay works harder and moves you closer to financial freedom. Lowering your interest rate lets you get there faster.

The Challenge

Review the interest rate on each debt. And as a bonus challenge, contact at least one creditor to see if you can get the interest rate lowered.

To help you get started, here is a sample script you can use when calling or emailing the creditor.

> Hello, My name is [Your Name], and I've been a cardholder since [year]. I'm working on reducing my balance and would like to request a review of my current interest rate.
>
> I've received offers from other companies with lower APRs, but I value my relationship with your company and would prefer to continue using this card. If possible, I'd appreciate being considered for a reduced interest rate or any available promotional or retention programs.
>
> Thank you for your time and assistance.

Reflection

Now that you've seen your interest rates clearly, what shifted for you? Write about the one insight that changes how you think about your debt and where you need to focus next. Did you call a creditor? What happened?

Your Waypoint Takeaway

Knowing your interest rates turns your debt plan into a strategy instead of a guess. It shows you where your money has the most power and helps you focus on the balances that matter most. Clarity here creates efficiency. And efficiency builds momentum.

DAY 14

Create a Debt Tracking System

A debt tracking system is your dashboard. Tracking isn't about perfection; it is about awareness and watching your progress.

It's the place where your numbers stop floating around in your head and finally land somewhere you can see, measure, and manage. When you track your debt, you turn a vague financial stressor into a clear, organized plan you can follow.

Most people carry their debt without really knowing how it moves. They make payments but don't see the impact. They feel overwhelmed but can't pinpoint why. A tracking system changes that. It shows you exactly where you stand, how far you've come, and what's left to conquer.

As you build your system, you'll notice patterns. You'll see which debts shrink quickly and which ones barely budge. You'll recognize how interest affects your progress. You'll spot the moments when your momentum grows, and the moments when it slips. This visibility gives you control. It turns your debt payoff journey into something you can steer, rather than something that steers you.

A tracking system also builds motivation. Every time you update it, you acknowledge your effort. You're celebrating small wins. You're reinforcing the habit of paying attention, and attention is what keeps you consistent. Over time, your tracking system becomes more than a tool. It becomes proof of your discipline, your strategy, and your commitment to change.

"Progress you can see becomes progress you want to continue."

Why This Matters

A debt tracking system matters because it keeps you informed and motivated. When you can see your balances, interest, and progress in one place, you make better decisions and stay focused on what truly moves the needle. Tracking turns your debt payoff plan into a measurable, manageable process, and measurable progress is what keeps you moving forward.

The Challenge

Create a visual tracker for your debt payoff.

A Simple Tracking System

Debt Name	Balance	Interest Rate	Minimum Payment	Last Payment Date	New Balance

How to Use It

- Once a month, update your balances.
- Record the last payment date *every* time you pay.
- Watch how the new balance changes.
- Highlight the debt you are focusing on first.
- Celebrate every decrease, even the tiny ones.

Reflection

Where will you keep your tracker? How will you use it to help you stay motivated?

Your Waypoint Takeaway

Tracking your debt gives you clarity, control, and momentum. When your numbers are organized and visible, your strategy becomes sharper, and your progress becomes real.

Celebrate Taking Control

This section was about turning the unknown into the understood. You gathered your numbers, named your barriers, reviewed your interest rates, and built a simple system to track your progress. Each step gives you a clearer picture of where you stand and what's been holding you back. That clarity is powerful. Why? Because once you can see your debt, you can finally start directing it instead of reacting to it.

You've moved from scattered information to organized insight. From avoidance to awareness. From feeling overwhelmed to feeling equipped. This is the shift that makes real change possible. Control doesn't come from paying off debt quickly; it comes from understanding your debt deeply. And now you do.

As you move forward, remember: clarity is your anchor. Control is your next step. You've built the foundation. Today, you are ready to build momentum.

And momentum is where clarity becomes confidence.

This next phase is about applying everything you've learned about your barriers, interest rates, tracking system, and new awareness. Then, putting it into motion in your real, everyday life. Debt confidence isn't theoretical. It's practical. It shows up in the choices you make, the habits you strengthen, and the way you respond when life throws you curveballs.

You're moving from understanding your debt to actively shaping it. From organizing your numbers to using them. From clarity to control, and now, from control to confident action.

This is where your strategy becomes a lived experience. This is where your plan progresses. This is where you start practicing debt confidence in real time.

Reflection

Now that you've organized your numbers, named your barriers, and built a system to track your debt, what feels different about the way you see your financial situation? Reflect on the moment in this section when clarity shifted into a sense of control, and how that shift prepares you to start using debt confidence in your real life.

Applying Debt Confidence in Real Life

Debt confidence becomes real the moment you start using it. Up to now, you've built clarity, created structure, and learned how your debt behaves. You've identified what holds you back and what moves you forward. That work wasn't theoretical. It was preparation. Now you're stepping into the part of the journey where your decisions, habits, and daily choices begin to reflect the confidence you've been building.

Applying debt confidence in real life isn't about perfection. It's about consistency. It's about choosing actions that align with your goals, even when life gets busy, stressful, or unpredictable. Confidence shows up in the way you plan your payments, the way you respond to setbacks, and the way you protect your progress. It's the quiet shift from "I hope this works" to "I know what to do next."

This phase is where your strategy becomes a lived experience. You'll practice making intentional choices, adjusting when things change, and staying grounded in the clarity you've earned. You're not just managing debt. You are shaping your financial future with purpose and awareness.

Debt confidence is a skill. And now, you're ready to use it.

DAY 15

Identify Your Credit Use Patterns

Your credit use tells a story. A story that you may not have realized you were writing.

Every swipe, every balance, and every moment you rely on credit creates a pattern. Some patterns are intentional, most are accidental, but all of them shape your financial reality.

Identifying your credit use patterns means stepping back and noticing how you use credit in daily life. Do you turn to it when stressed or overwhelmed? Use it for convenience purchases? Rely on it when cash flow feels tight? Or carry balances simply because you never paused to see how they formed?

When you examine your patterns, you start to see the truth behind your balances. You notice where spending creeps higher, when credit becomes a habit, and which emotional triggers drive your choices. Once you see those patterns clearly, you can begin to change them.

This step is not about blame. It is about awareness. Patterns run quietly in the background, but once you identify them, you can interrupt them, replace them, and build habits that support your goals.

"Patterns review opportunities for change."

Why This Matters

Your credit use patterns determine how your balances grow, how your budget feels, and how much financial pressure you carry each month. When you understand these patterns, you can spot the habits that keep you stuck, reduce the spending that creates unnecessary debt, and make choices that align with your long-term goals. Awareness turns credit from a reactive tool into a strategic one. Once you make this shift, you can protect your progress.

The Challenge

Identify when and why you reach for credit.

Reflection

Which credit use patterns stood out to you? Reflect on whether they help you or hold you back. Then identify one beneficial pattern you can strengthen and one harmful pattern you can begin to change.

Your Waypoint Takeaway

Your credit use isn't random. It follows patterns. When you identify those patterns, you gain the power to change them. Clarity here helps you break habits that create debt and build habits that support financial confidence.

DAY 16
Take a Credit Break Today

A single day won't change your entire financial life, but it can change your relationship with credit.

You wake up already knowing today will feel different. There's a quiet resolve in the air because today, you decide to interrupt a pattern that's been running on autopilot. All day long, you move through your routine with a new kind of awareness. Every moment you would normally reach for a card for that quick tap at the gas pump, the impulse snack, the "I'll just put it on credit" convenience, becomes a pause, a choice, a reset.

And with each choice, you feel something shift.

It's not about deprivation. It's about reclaiming control. Today, you're proving to yourself that you can meet your needs without leaning on borrowed money. You're reminding your brain what it feels like to spend intentionally instead of reflexively. You're giving your future self a break from the interest, the balances, the mental clutter.

A single day won't change your entire financial life. But it *will* change your relationship with credit, and that's where transformation begins.

"A day without credit builds trust in yourself."

Why This Matters

Taking a one-day credit break interrupts the cycle of unconscious spending and helps you see your habits clearly. Research on credit-related observances highlights how easily revolving balances grow when credit becomes the default instead of a deliberate tool. High-interest debt can quietly accumulate, increasing financial stress and limiting long-term goals like homeownership or retirement.

A temporary 24-hour pause gives you space to:

- Notice how often you rely on credit for convenience rather than necessity.
- Reduce the risk of adding new charges that contribute to long-term balances.
- Strengthen your ability to live within your actual cash flow, a core step in regaining control over debt.
- Build confidence that you *can* operate without leaning on credit as a safety net.

The Challenge

Avoid using credit today. Pay with cash, debit, or give yourself permission to say, "No, I don't need to purchase this today."

Reflection

What did you learn about your habits today?

Your Waypoint Takeaway

A credit break is a reset button. It's a small, strategic pause that reminds you that credit is a tool, not a lifeline. By choosing one day of cash-only living, you strengthen your discipline, reduce the chance of new debt, and build trust in your own ability to manage your money with intention. Today's pause becomes tomorrow's progress.

DAY 17

Identify Your Debt Strengths

For most people, listing their financial weaknesses is easy. Overspending, fear, avoidance, and inconsistency are easy to identify, but your strengths? They take a little more thought and intention to see.

Today is about flipping the script.

You sit down with your notebook, expecting this to feel awkward. But as you start writing, something surprising happens, and you realize you *do* have strengths. Real ones. Maybe you've never named them, but they've been quietly shaping your financial decisions all along.

Maybe you're disciplined once you commit. Maybe you're resourceful when money gets tight. Maybe you're determined because you've survived things that would have broken other people. Maybe you're organized, or thoughtful, or patient, or persistent.

Debt doesn't erase your strengths. Debt doesn't define your character. Debt doesn't cancel out the skills you already have.

Today is about recognizing the parts of you that will make your debt-free journey possible. Because you're not starting from zero. You are starting from experience, resilience, and capability.

Naming your strengths isn't bragging. It's preparation.

"Your strengths are the foundation of your confidence."

Why This Matters

Identifying your debt strengths builds confidence and clarity, the two things research consistently shows are essential for long-term financial behavior change. When people understand their own capabilities, they're more likely to stick with a plan, make consistent payments, and avoid self-sabotage driven by shame or fear (of success or failure).

Debt payoff isn't just about math. It's about mindset.

Recognizing your strengths helps you:

- Shift from "I'm bad with money" to "I have tools I can use."
- Build motivation rooted in identity, not fear.
- See yourself as capable, not broken.
- Leverage what already works for you instead of trying to become someone else.
- Create a payoff strategy that aligns with your natural tendencies — which increases follow-through.

People succeed financially when they work *with* their strengths, not against them.

The Challenge

List three strengths you bring to your debt journey.

____

____

____

Reflection

How hard was it to identify your strengths? What surprised you about yourself today?

Your Waypoint Takeaway

You already have what you need to begin. Your strengths are the engine of your debt-free journey. Your discipline, resilience, creativity, consistency, or courage will help you succeed on this journey. When you name your strengths, you activate them.

Today's work isn't about fixing what's wrong. It's about recognizing what's right.

DAY 18

Create a Pause Button on Credit

Pause for at least 10 minutes before using credit today.

You don't realize how automatic credit has become until you try to interrupt it.

Today's challenge isn't about eliminating credit. It's about slowing it down, and creating a moment between the impulse and the swipe.

A pause button. A breath. A checkpoint.

You move through your day noticing how often your hand drifts toward a card without a second thought. It's muscle memory. Convenience. Habit. But today, you stop yourself. You ask a question. You create space. And that space is powerful.

In that pause, you see the purchase more clearly. You feel the difference between *want* and *need*. You recognize when you're spending out of boredom, stress, or routine. You notice when credit is covering up something deeper, like fatigue, frustration, or fear of facing your actual cash flow.

The pause doesn't judge you. It simply gives you time to choose.

And with each pause, you feel your confidence grow. You're not just reacting. You're deciding. You're reclaiming control over the part of your financial life that used to run on autopilot.

Today, you didn't eliminate credit. You made it conscious.

"A pause creates clarity."

Why This Matters

Creating a pause button on credit is one of the most effective ways to disrupt unconscious spending patterns. Behavioral research shows that even a two-second interruption between impulse and action can significantly reduce automatic behaviors, especially those tied to convenience, habit, or emotional triggers.

A pause helps you:

- Shift from reflexive spending to intentional decision-making.
- Reduce the likelihood of adding new debt that doesn't align with your goals.
- Catch emotional spending before it becomes a balance you regret.
- Strengthen your ability to evaluate purchases based on cash flow, not convenience.
- Build trust in your own judgment — a core component of long-term financial confidence.

Credit isn't the enemy. Unconscious credit use is.

The pause button gives you control of the steering wheel.

The Challenge

Add a pause point before any credit use today.

Reflection

What did your pause reveal about your habits today?

Your Waypoint Takeaway

A pause button is a power move. It turns credit from an automatic habit into a deliberate choice. Every time you pause, you reinforce your ability to act with intention instead of impulse. Today's pause becomes tomorrow's progress, one conscious decision at a time.

DAY 19
Create a Debt-Free Vision

A debt-free vision is a compass. It points you toward the life you're building, one intentional step at a time.

Close your eyes for a moment and imagine your life without debt.

Not the numbers. Not the statements. Not the balances. The *life*.

What does it feel like to wake up without that weight on your chest? What choices are open in a debt-free future? What dreams stop feeling unrealistic and start feeling possible? What kind of calm settles into your day when your money finally belongs to you?

Today's challenge is about stepping into that future long enough to see it clearly.

You sit with your notebook and begin sketching out the version of yourself who is debt-free. Maybe you picture a home that feels peaceful. Maybe you imagine traveling without guilt. Maybe you see yourself saving with confidence, giving generously, or simply breathing easier.

As you write, something shifts. Your vision stops being a fantasy and starts becoming a direction.

This isn't about pretending your debt doesn't exist. It's about remembering why you're doing the work, and who you're becoming because of it.

"A clear vision makes daily choices easier."

Why This Matters

Creating a debt-free vision strengthens your motivation and anchors your financial decisions in purpose. Behavioral research consistently shows that people stick with long-term goals when they can visualize the outcome, not just the process. A clear vision reduces fear of moving forward because it gives your brain something to move *toward*, not just something to move *away from*.

A debt-free vision helps you:

- Connect your daily choices to a meaningful future.
- Replace fear with clarity because you are not just paying off debt, you're building a life.
- Stay focused when progress feels slow or discouraging.
- Make decisions that align with your long-term goals instead of short-term impulses.
- Strengthen your identity as someone capable of financial change.

Debt payoff is easier when you know what freedom looks like.

The Challenge

Write a 1 – 3 year vision for your debt-free life.

Reflection

Which part of your debt-free future feels like it will change you the most? Write about the moment in your vision that makes you feel stronger, freer, or more fully *you!*

Your Waypoint Takeaway

Your debt-free vision is your North Star. It reminds you who you're becoming and why the work matters. When you can see your future clearly, every payment, every pause, every intentional choice becomes part of a bigger story. It becomes your story of confidence, freedom, and financial peace.

DAY 20
Identify Your "Just This Once" Debt Patterns

You know that phrase! You have said it, possibly more than once.

"Just this once."

It's the quiet permission slip that sneaks debt into your life as a harmless exception. It is the small purchase, a quick fix, a moment of convenience. You tell yourself it's no big deal because it's only this one time.

But today, you're looking closer.

You start noticing when "just this once" appears. Maybe it's when you're tired, stressed, or feel you deserve something after a long day. Maybe it's when you don't want to face your actual cash flow.

You begin to see the pattern: "Just this once" isn't random. It's predictable. And once you see it, you can't unsee it.

Today isn't about shame. It's about awareness. You're mapping the triggers, situations, and stories that make credit feel like the easy button. You're learning how your mind negotiates with your goals and how small exceptions quietly add up.

"Just this Once
becomes a habit when you are not paying attention."

Why This Matters

"Just this once" spending is one of the most common ways debt grows, not through big emergencies, but through small, repeated exceptions. People are more likely to break financial rules when they believe the break is temporary or justified. But temporary exceptions often become recurring patterns.

Identifying these moments helps you:

- Understand the emotional triggers behind your spending.
- Interrupt the cycle before it becomes new debt.
- Replace impulsive exceptions with intentional decisions.
- Strengthen your confidence by recognizing where your boundaries slip.
- Build a debt payoff plan that accounts for real-life stressors and habits.

Awareness is the first step toward control. Once you see your patterns, you can change them.

Awareness prevents you from drifting away from your goals.

The Challenge

Identify one area where "just this once" leads to debt.

Reflection

What emotions or behaviors are driving your "just this once" excuses?

Your Waypoint Takeaway

Your "just this once" moments aren't accidents. They are patterns. When you identify them, you reclaim the power to choose differently. Today's awareness becomes tomorrow's discipline, and discipline becomes the foundation of your debt-free future.

DAY 21

Build a Debt-Friendly Environment

Your environment shapes your behaviors more than your intentions ever will.

You've done a lot of internal work of identifying patterns, naming strengths, and creating a vision. Today shifts the focus to something just as important: the world around you.

You start noticing the little things that nudge you toward spending. The saved credit card in your browser. The "Buy Now" button that's always one click away. The store you walk into when you're bored. The social media posts that promise deals you weren't even looking for. The apps that make it easy to spend without thinking.

None of these things are wrong. But they're powerful.

Today's challenge is to redesign your surroundings so they support your debt-free goals rather than pull you away from them. You remove temptations, add reminders, and create systems that make the right choice the easy choice.

Maybe you will delete a saved card. Maybe you will unsubscribe from a few emails. Maybe you will reorganize your wallet so that cash or debit comes first. Maybe you set up a visual reminder of your debt-free vision where you'll see it before you spend.

As you make these small changes, you feel something shift. Your environment starts working *with* you instead of against you.

This isn't about restriction. It's about alignment and shaping your world to match the future you're building.

"Your environment should support your goals."

Why This Matters

People are far more likely to follow through on goals when their environment supports the desired behavior. Debt-friendly environments reduce friction, lower temptation, and make intentional choices easier to sustain.

A supportive environment helps you:

- Reduce impulse spending triggered by convenience or habit.
- Interrupt "just this once" moments before they become new debt.
- Strengthen your ability to stick to your plan without relying on willpower alone.
- Keep your debt-free vision visible and emotionally present.
- Build consistency — the foundation of long-term financial change.

Your surroundings influence your spending more than motivation, discipline, or good intentions. When you shape your environment, you shape your outcomes.

The Challenge

Make one environmental change that reduces credit use today.

Reflection

What change did you make today? Did you stop carrying credit cards? Did you (literally) freeze your credit card (I did this once. I put the credit card in a bowl of water and kept it in the freezer. To use it, the water had to melt before I could see the numbers.)? Did you delete credit cards from online accounts?

Your Waypoint Takeaway

A debt-friendly environment is a quiet form of self-support. It removes friction, reduces temptation, and keeps your goals front and center. When your world is set up for success, every choice becomes easier, and your debt-free future becomes more attainable.

DAY 22

Practice a Low-Spend Day

Today, practice no spending money and redirect what you would have spent to paying down debt.

Today feels lighter from the moment you begin. Not because you're depriving yourself, but because you're choosing simplicity. You are choosing to take a day where spending steps back and awareness steps forward.

You move through your routine, noticing how much of your daily spending isn't about true need. It's a habit, a convenience, or a treat you deserve. It could be a moment of boredom. But today, you're practicing something different: a day where you spend only on what's essential.

You pack your lunch instead of grabbing something on the go. You make coffee at home. You skip the impulse stop at the store. You use what you already have. You plan ahead just enough to keep the day running smoothly.

And with each intentional choice, you feel a quiet sense of control settling in.

A low-spend day isn't about restriction. It's about clarity. It's about proving to yourself that you can create space in your budget without feeling stressed or deprived. It's about learning how much of your spending is optional, and how capable you are of choosing differently.

By the end of the day, you're not proud because you spent less. You're proud because you spent money *on purpose*.

"Every low-spend day strengthens your momentum."

Why This Matters

Low-spend days are powerful because they build financial confidence through small, repeatable wins. Temporary constraints, when chosen intentionally, help people reset spending habits, reduce emotional purchases, and reconnect with their actual cash flow.

Practicing a low-spend day helps you:

- Interrupt automatic spending patterns.
- Reduce "just this once" purchases that quietly add up.
- Strengthen your ability to plan ahead and anticipate needs.
- Build momentum toward larger debt-free goals.
- Experience what financial calm feels like, even for one day.

It's not about saving a huge amount. It's about proving you can create breathing room whenever you choose.

The Challenge

Plan ahead for today (or tomorrow) to have a low-spend day. Put the systems in place so that you don't have to spend because you "forgot" or were in a hurry.

Reflection

What did today mean to you?

Your Waypoint Takeaway

A low-spend day is a reset button for your wallet and your mindset. It reminds you that you can control your spending without feeling restricted, and that small, intentional choices build the foundation for long-term financial freedom.

Bask in Your New-Found Confidence

Over the past several days, you shifted from understanding your debt to *actively practicing confidence in real time*. Each day, you were asked to make small, intentional choices that strengthened your awareness, your discipline, and your belief in your ability to manage debt with clarity and control.

You began by identifying your debt patterns, taking a credit break, proving you can meet your needs without leaning on borrowed money. You learned to pause before using credit, interrupting the automatic habits that quietly create balances. You created a debt-free vision, giving your brain a future to move toward instead of a problem to run from.

You identified your debt strengths, recognizing the qualities that will carry you through this journey. You uncovered your "just this once" patterns, revealing the emotional triggers that lead to exceptions that become habits. You built a debt-friendly environment, shaping your surroundings to support your goals rather than pull you away from them.

And finally, you practiced a low-spend day, experiencing what intentional, simplified spending feels like, and discovering how much control you can create with small, thoughtful choices.

Together, these challenges formed a powerful shift: You moved from reacting to your debt to *actively shaping* your financial behavior. You proved that confidence isn't something you wait for. Instead, confidence is something you practice.

Reflection

Look back at the past week. Which shift in your real-life behavior has strengthened your debt confidence the most? How has that change begun to reshape the way you move through your financial life?

Building Long-Term Debt Confidence

Now that you've applied debt confidence in your daily life, you're ready for the next phase: building long-term confidence that lasts beyond the moment, the day, or the challenge.

Debt confidence isn't about paying off everything overnight. It is about building a long-term identity as someone who understands their debt, manages it with clarity, and moves toward freedom with confidence. This week, you step into that identity.

This next section will help you strengthen consistency, deepen your habits, and create systems that support your debt-free identity for the long haul. You've built momentum. Now you'll build endurance.

Notes

DAY 23

Identify Your Long-Term Debt Priorities

You don't need to tackle everything at once. You can take the time to focus on what matters most.

Long-term debt priorities are commitments that stretch beyond the next few months. They shape your financial landscape for years and influence your stability, stress levels, and future opportunities. Identifying them is not just listing what you owe. It is deciding what matters most to your future self.

This step pulls you out of the day-to-day grind and into the bigger picture. Which debts carry emotional weight? Which limit your choices? Which, if eliminated, would create the greatest relief? Long-term priorities often include mortgages, student loans, auto loans, or large credit balances, but the real priority is defined by the impact each debt has on your life.

This matters because long-term debt easily becomes background noise. You get used to it and stop imagining life without it. Bringing these debts back into focus helps you reclaim agency. You stop reacting and start directing, and you see how long-term decisions connect to long-term confidence.

This clarity also keeps you from drifting into short-term fixes that feel productive but do not create real progress. When you know your long-term priorities, every payment and every strategy becomes intentional. You are building momentum toward a future where debt no longer defines your limits.

"Priorities protect your energy."

Why This Matters

Long-term debt priorities matter because they determine the direction of your financial future. When you know which debts carry the biggest impact, you stop scattering your energy across everything you owe and start applying it where it creates real movement. Without clear priorities, long-term debt becomes background noise. Noise that is always there, always draining, never improving. With priorities, every payment becomes a strategic step toward stability, freedom, and long-term confidence. This clarity keeps you from drifting and ensures your effort builds momentum instead of frustration.

The Challenge

List your top three long-term det priorities.

Reflection

Which priority feels most important? Any why does it matter to you?

Your Waypoint Takeaway

Long-term debt priorities anchor your confidence. When you know which obligations matter most to your future stability, you stop treating debt as a collection of bills and start treating it as a strategic path forward. Clarity today becomes freedom tomorrow.

DAY 24
Build a Debt Ladder

A debt ladder breaks your big goals into smaller milestones. And small milestones are easier to achieve, leading to more satisfaction.

A debt ladder is your step-by-step path out of debt. It provides a clear sequence that shows exactly what you'll tackle first, next, and after that. Instead of trying to solve everything at once, the ladder gives you a structured climb. Each rung represents a specific action you can take, and each step builds momentum for the one that follows.

When you build your debt ladder, you're creating a plan that matches your reality. You're choosing the order that makes sense for your life, your stress level, and your long-term goals. Maybe you start with the smallest balance to build confidence. Maybe you start with the highest interest rate to save money. Maybe you start with the debt that carries the most emotional weight. The ladder doesn't judge your priorities. It allows you to organize them.

The power of a debt ladder is that it makes progress visible. Every rung you climb is a win. Every step forward reinforces your discipline. And every completed rung proves that you're capable of moving from one stage to the next. Instead of feeling overwhelmed by everything you owe, you focus on the next step, then the next.

A debt ladder isn't just a plan. It's a mindset shift. It's the moment you stop trying to leap to the top and start climbing with intention. You're not hoping your debt will disappear. You're building the path that gets you there.

"Small steps make big goals possible."

Why This Matters

A debt ladder matters because it replaces chaos with clarity. Without a ladder, debt feels like a tangled list of balances competing for your attention. With a ladder, you know exactly where to start and exactly what comes next. This structure keeps you from stalling, second-guessing, or bouncing between debts without making real progress. A ladder turns your effort into momentum — and momentum is what carries you from the first rung all the way to the top.

The Challenge

Look back at your priority ranking list from Day 9. Divide at least one debt into 3 – 5 milestones.

Reflection

When you look at the debt ladder you created, which rung feels like the most meaningful step for your future confidence, and what does taking that step reveal about the way you want to move through your financial life?

Your Waypoint Takeaway

A debt ladder gives you direction. When you organize your debts into a clear sequence, you stop feeling overwhelmed and start feeling capable. One rung at a time, you build confidence, discipline, and measurable progress toward freedom.

DAY 25

Identify Your Money Strengths

Creating a debt safety plan isn't about expecting disaster. It's about acknowledging reality and preparing for it with confidence.

A debt safety plan is your protection strategy. It is the set of actions you put in place so your debt payoff journey can survive real life. Because life will happen. A surprise bill, a medical copay, a car repair, a schedule change, a paycheck disruption. Without a safety plan, any one of these moments can knock you off track and send you right back into the cycle you're trying to escape.

You start by identifying the situations most likely to derail your progress. Then you decide how you'll respond before those moments arrive. Maybe it's a small buffer you maintain. Maybe it's a rule about pausing extra payments instead of stopping them entirely. Maybe it's a communication plan for yourself, a reminder of what you're working toward and why you don't want to lose momentum.

A safety plan gives you options. It gives you structure. It gives you a way to stay committed even when circumstances shift. Instead of reacting with stress or frustration, you respond with intention. You already know your next move, and that clarity keeps you grounded.

Most importantly, a debt safety plan protects your confidence. It ensures that one setback doesn't become a spiral. It keeps your progress intact. It reminds you that you're building a financial life that can bend without breaking.

"A plan protects your progress."

Why This Matters

A debt safety plan matters because progress is fragile without protection. Even small disruptions can undo weeks or months of effort if you don't have a plan for how to handle them. With a safety plan, you stay in control. You prevent setbacks from becoming patterns. You maintain momentum even when life gets unpredictable. This preparation strengthens your discipline, reduces stress, and keeps your long-term strategy moving forward.

The Challenge

Write a plan for handling surprise expenses without credit. To build your plan, walk through these steps:

1. Identify the most likely surprise expenses. Think about the things that have disrupted your budget in the past, such as car repairs, medical bills, appliance failures, or any other surprise. List the top three that are most realistic for your life.
2. Choose your non-credit response strategy. What options do you have to cover the expense without using a credit card?
3. Write your "If this happens, I will . . ." plan. Turn each scenario into a clear action statement. For example: If my car needs repair, I will use my emergency buffer first, then pause extra payments for one cycle, and rebuild the buffer before resuming my debt ladder.
4. Add a confidence anchor. Write one sentence that reminds you why avoiding credit matters for your long-term stability.

"A plan protects your progress."

Why This Matters

A debt safety plan matters because progress is fragile without protection. Even small disruptions can undo weeks or months of effort if you don't have a plan for how to handle them. With a safety plan, you stay in control. You prevent setbacks from becoming patterns. You maintain momentum even when life gets unpredictable. This preparation strengthens your discipline, reduces stress, and keeps your long-term strategy moving forward.

The Challenge

Write a plan for handling surprise expenses without credit. To build your plan, walk through these steps:

1. Identify the most likely surprise expenses. Think about the things that have happened to you most in the past: car repairs, medical bills, appliances, pet issues, or any other [illegible]. List the top [illegible] most likely for your life.
2. Choose your go-to option for each scenario. What options do you have to cover the expense without using credit?
3. Write your "If this happens, I will…" plan. Turn each scenario into a clear action statement. For example: "If my car needs repair, I will use my emergency fund first, then pause extra payments for one cycle, and rebuild the buffer before resuming my snowball."
4. Add a confidence anchor. Write one sentence that reminds you why avoiding credit matters for your long-term stability.

Reflection

How can you implement your Debt Safety Plan?

Your Waypoint Takeaway

A debt safety plan is your anchor for stability. When you prepare for the moments that could derail your progress, you protect your confidence and your momentum. You're not just paying off debt. You're building a resilient financial path that can withstand real life.

DAY 26

Create a Debt Identity Statement

A debt identity statement is a declaration of who you are becoming in your financial life.

It's not about the numbers you owe. It's about the person you choose to be while you pay them off. Debt can quietly shape your self-image, making you feel behind or stuck. A debt identity statement interrupts that pattern and gives you a new narrative to stand on.

When you write your statement, you define your role in this journey. You choose words that reflect your strength, discipline, and direction. You name the qualities you want to embody as you climb your debt ladder and build long-term stability. Whether your statement centers on resilience, consistency, courage, clarity, or confidence, it becomes your anchor when progress feels slow or setbacks feel heavy.

This isn't about pretending debt is easy. It's about refusing to let it define your identity. Your statement becomes the voice you return to when doubt appears and the mindset you practice as you make payments, adjust your budget, or handle surprise expenses. It becomes the story you tell yourself about your capability, not your limitations.

A debt identity statement is small but powerful. It marks the moment you stop seeing yourself as someone trying to get out of debt and start seeing yourself as someone actively building financial freedom, one intentional choice at a time.

"Identity drives behavior."

Why This Matters

Your identity drives your behavior. When you see yourself as capable, disciplined, and committed, you make choices that reinforce those qualities. Without a clear identity, it's easy to slip into old habits, lose momentum, or let setbacks derail your progress. A debt identity statement strengthens your mindset, protects your confidence, and keeps your actions aligned with the person you're becoming. It transforms debt payoff from a task into a personal evolution.

The Challenge

Write a statement describing the kind of debt manager you are becoming.

Reflection

What identity shift feels most powerful?

Your Waypoint Takeaway

Your debt identity statement is your compass. When you define who you are on this journey, you make decisions with clarity and confidence. You're not just paying off debt. You're becoming the version of yourself who finishes the climb.

DAY 27

Strengthen Your Environment for Long-Term Confidence

Long-term confidence doesn't grow in isolation.

Confidence grows in the environment you build around your financial life. It comes from the habits you practice, the tools you rely on, the people you trust, and the spaces where you make decisions. When your environment supports your goals, confidence is easier to maintain. When it works against you, even strong motivation can fade.

Strengthening your environment means shaping conditions that help you stay consistent. It is choosing routines that keep your debt ladder visible, organizing your financial information so you are not scrambling, and surrounding yourself with reminders of progress instead of triggers that pull you backward. It includes physical, digital, and emotional cues that make your decisions feel grounded rather than stressful.

This is not about perfection. It is about alignment. When your environment matches your goals, you reduce friction. You make the right choices easier and the wrong ones harder. You build systems that support you when motivation dips or life gets busy. You create a financial world that reinforces your identity, priorities, and long-term direction.

Strengthening your environment is a quiet discipline. It is the behind-the-scenes work that makes confidence sustainable and turns intentions into lived experience — not just for today, but for the future you are building.

"Your environment should make confidence the easy choice."

Why This Matters

Your environment influences your behavior more than willpower ever will. When your surroundings support your financial goals, you stay consistent with less effort. When they don't, even strong intentions can slip. Strengthening your environment reduces stress, prevents backtracking, and protects the confidence you've worked hard to build. It ensures that your long-term debt strategy isn't fighting against the world you live in; it's supported by it.

The Challenge

Make one environmental change that supports long-term confidence. For example, remove stored credit cards from your digital wallet and online accounts. What change did you make?

Reflection

Why is this environmental change important to you?

Your Waypoint Takeaway

A strong environment enables long-term confidence. When you intentionally shape the space around your financial life, you reinforce your progress, reduce friction, and create conditions where your best decisions become your normal decisions.

DAY 28

Celebrate Your Debt Wins

Debt payoff is a long journey, and long journeys need moments of celebration.

Every payment you make, every balance you reduce, every habit you strengthen is a win, not because it's perfect, but because it moves you forward. Too often, people dismiss their progress because it feels small or slow. But small wins are what build big change.

Celebrating your debt wins is about acknowledging the effort behind the numbers. It recognizes the discipline it took to make that payment, the courage it took to face your balances, and the consistency it took to stay committed when life pulled at your attention. These wins are proof that you're doing the work. They're evidence that you're becoming the person who finishes what they start.

When you celebrate your wins, you reinforce your identity. You remind yourself that progress is happening, even if the finish line feels far away. You give your brain the motivation it needs to keep going. You turn your debt journey from something heavy into something hopeful — a series of steps you can be proud of.

Celebration doesn't have to be big. It can be a moment of reflection, a note in your journal, a quiet acknowledgment that you showed up for yourself today. What matters is that you pause long enough to recognize your momentum. Because momentum grows when you honor it.

"Celebration reinforces the habits you want to keep."

Why This Matters

Celebrating your debt wins matters because motivation fades without reinforcement. When you acknowledge your progress, you strengthen your confidence, increase your consistency, and make it easier to stay committed over time. Celebration turns effort into energy. It keeps you from feeling stuck, overwhelmed, or disconnected from your own success. Most importantly, it transforms your debt payoff journey from a grind into a series of meaningful victories.

The Challenge

List five debt wins from the past 28 days.

Reflection

Why do these wins feel most meaningful? How did you celebrate?

Your Waypoint Takeaway

Your debt wins deserve recognition. When you celebrate your progress — no matter how small — you fuel your confidence, reinforce your discipline, and build the momentum that carries you forward. Every win is a step toward freedom, and every step counts.

DAY 29

Create a Long-Term Debt Vision

Debt payoff can feel slow, and slow progress can make you forget why you started. A long-term vision brings that future back into focus.

When you create your vision, you're giving yourself permission to imagine what life looks like without the weight of debt. Maybe it's the calm of knowing your paycheck belongs to you. Maybe it's the ability to save without fear, travel without guilt, or make choices without hesitation. Maybe it's simply waking up without that quiet pressure in the back of your mind. Your vision doesn't have to be dramatic. It just has to be honest.

This vision becomes your compass. It's the reminder you return to when motivation dips or setbacks appear, trying to force you down the wrong path. It's the story that keeps you grounded when the process feels long. It's the emotional fuel behind every intentional choice you make. When you can see your future clearly, your present decisions become more purposeful. You're not just paying off debt; instead, you're moving toward a life that feels lighter, stronger, and more aligned with who you want to be.

A long-term debt vision is a promise to your future self. It's the moment you stop focusing only on what you're leaving behind and start focusing on what you're moving toward.

"A clear vision is your daily roadmap, making choices easier."

Why This Matters

A long-term debt vision matters because clarity strengthens commitment. When you know what freedom looks like, you're more likely to stay consistent, make intentional choices, and push through discouraging moments. Without a vision, debt payoff becomes a task. With a vision, it becomes a transformation. Your brain needs something to move toward — not just something to escape. A clear vision keeps your motivation alive and your confidence growing.

The Challenge

Write a 1 – 3 year vision of your journey. Where do you want to be and how are you going to get there?

Reflection

What part of your vision excites you the most?

Your Waypoint Takeaway

Your long-term debt vision is your North Star. When you can see the future you're building, every payment becomes a step toward possibility, not pressure. Clarity today creates confidence tomorrow.

DAY 30

Claim Your Identity as a Confident Debt Manager

This is the moment where everything you've practiced, learned, and strengthened comes together.

Over the past 30 days, you've built habits, clarified priorities, created systems, and reshaped how you think about debt. But the biggest transformation isn't in your balances. It's in your identity. You've become someone who manages debt with clarity and confidence.

Claiming your identity as a confident debt manager means recognizing who you are now. You're directing your debt instead of reacting to it. You're equipped rather than overwhelmed. You've built tools, routines, and a mindset that support you. Confidence isn't something you wait to feel once the debt is gone. It's something you practice as you pay it off.

This identity changes how you show up in your financial life. You make decisions from strength, respond to setbacks with strategy, celebrate progress, and trust yourself to follow through. That trust carries into every financial choice beyond this challenge.

Claiming your identity lasts long after balances shift. It becomes the foundation for every future financial goal and the story you continue to write.

You didn't just finish 30 days. You became someone new in the process.

"You are not your debt. You are the one in control of it."

Why This Matters

Identity drives behavior. When you see yourself as a confident debt manager, you make choices that reinforce that confidence. You stay consistent. You stay intentional. You stay grounded. Without claiming this identity, it's easy to slip back into old patterns or let doubt take over when progress feels slow. With it, you carry forward the discipline, clarity, and strength you've built — not just for debt payoff, but for every financial decision ahead. This identity is your long-term advantage.

The Challenge

Write your declaration of your identity as a confident debt manager.

Reflection

What part of this journey means the most to you?

Your Waypoint Takeaway

Confidence is now part of your financial identity. When you claim who you've become, you protect your progress, strengthen your momentum, and step into a future where you manage your money with clarity, purpose, and self-trust.

Strengthening Your Long-Term Debt Mindset

The work you did this week is a turning point in your debt journey. You've moved beyond strategies and tools and stepped into something deeper, the mindset and identity that make long-term confidence possible. You've built systems that support you, shaped an environment that strengthens you, and claimed the qualities that define who you are becoming. This is where debt management stops being a reaction and becomes a practice. It is your choice. You control the direction.

You've learned how to protect your progress, celebrate your wins, and anchor your decisions in a vision that feels real and motivating. You've proven that confidence isn't something you wait to feel at the end of your journey. It's something you build through consistent, intentional action. You now have the clarity to understand your path and the control to walk it with purpose.

As you move forward, carry this identity with you. Let it guide your decisions, steady your momentum, and remind you that you are capable of shaping your financial future. You're not just managing debt. You're managing it with confidence, direction, and strength.

You're ready for what comes next.

FINAL REFLECTION

Your Money Story Is Changing

You've spent this section strengthening the systems, habits, and identity that support long-term confidence related to debt. You've shaped your environment, clarified your vision, and practiced seeing yourself as someone who manages debt with intention instead of stress. Now it's time to step back and reflect on the transformation underneath all that work

Reflection

When you look at the way you think, act, and respond to your debt now, what evidence do you see that you're becoming a confident debt manager, and how does that new identity change the way you imagine your financial future?

The Next Journey

You've reached the end of this challenge, but you haven't reached the end of your growth. Over these thirty days, you've built more than a plan. You've built a new way of seeing yourself, your money, and your future. You've learned how to move with intention instead of reaction, clarity instead of confusion, and confidence instead of fear. You've proven that you can take control of your financial life one deliberate step at a time.

But this book was never meant to be the finish line. It was meant to be the foundation.

Your next journey begins with the identity you've claimed here, the identity of someone who manages debt with strength, direction, and self-trust. Now you get to carry that identity into the next phase of your financial life. Maybe it's building savings with purpose. Maybe it's creating long-term stability. Maybe it's about designing a future that reflects your values, goals, and vision for the life you want to live.

Whatever comes next, you're not starting from scratch. You're starting from confidence.

The tools you've built, the habits you've strengthened, and the mindset you've shaped will follow you into every financial decision ahead. You've already done the hard work of becoming someone who shows up for their future. Now you get to expand that future, step by step, with the same clarity and courage you practiced here.

This journey ends so the next one can begin — and you're ready for it.

Upcoming challenges in the series will guide you through topics like:

- 30 Days to Savings Momentum: Creating Systems That Make Saving Automatic and Sustainable

- 30 Days to Smarter Spending: Reshaping Habits, Triggers, and Patterns So Your Money Supports Your Values
- 30 Days to Financial Resilience: Preparing for Emergencies, Uncertainty, and Life's Inevitable Curveballs

Each challenge stands alone, but together they form a full roadmap—a series of waypoints that help you build a financial life that feels stable, intentional, and yours.

You've proven you can commit. You've proven you can grow. Now you get to choose your next waypoint.

Your journey continues from here.